R. Furneaux Jordan

Aug 1948

# VICTORIAN ARCHITECTURE

# AN INTRODUCTION TO
# Victorian
# Architecture

## HUGH CASSON

LONDON : ART AND TECHNICS : 1948

# INTRODUCTIONS TO ARCHITECTURE

### GENERAL EDITOR: HUGH CASSON, MA, ARIBA

★

REGENCY ARCHITECTURE by Paul Reilly
GEORGIAN ARCHITECTURE (2 vols) by Professor A. E. Richardson, RA
GOTHIC REVIVAL by Edwin Smith
VICTORIAN ARCHITECTURE by Hugh Casson, MA, ARIBA
MODERN ARCHITECTURE by Neville Conder, ARIBA

*First published* 1948 *by*
ART AND TECHNICS LTD 58 FRITH STREET LONDON W1
*and printed in Great Britain by*
SHENVAL PRESS LTD LONDON AND HERTFORD

# PREFACE

IGNORANCE, IT HAS BEEN SAID, is a prerequisite of the historian. This is particularly true of anyone who attempts to survey, however superficially, the achievements of the nineteenth century. The material at his hand is so overwhelming in bulk and so bewildering in texture and colour, that all he can do is pick over the tumbled debris of this vast quarry, and select at random a few stones which, when held up to the light, may reveal something of the nature of the complex mass from which they came.

This book does not claim to be more than a handful of such stones, all of them, it should be made clear, dislodged by the pickaxes of previous investigators. Those who look for original research or detailed survey must await those heavier volumes which it is the intention of the author to read as soon as they appear. For appear they certainly will. The Victorian age is the next one due, in the normal process, for the study, analysis—perhaps even the over-valuation, which has recently been accorded the Regency period. It is hoped, however, that this modest survey will act as an introduction to those more complete studies which are to come, and that meanwhile it will help to stimulate the respect, interest, even the affection, which the fabulous architecture of this truly fabulous age so emphatically deserves.

# CONTENTS

★

# THE ILLUSTRATIONS

## IN THE TEXT

## THE PLATES

★

# ACKNOWLEDGMENTS

All photographs are from the library of the National Buildings Record except:

Pages 49, 63, 74, 89, 96: photograph Hugh Veysey

Page 50: reproduced from the *Architect and Building News*, 1860

Page 51 *bottom*: by permission of the Press Division, Admiralty

Pages 51 *top*, 57 *top*: copyright Warburg Institute

Pages 56, 57 *bottom*: photograph Herbert Felton

Pages 52 *top*, 54, 60, 61, 80 *top*, 94: (photographs John Piper), all copyright Architectural Press Ltd

Page 53: copyright Professor A. E. Richardson. Photograph Brownings, Exeter

Page 62 *top*: copyright Oxford Public Library

Page 66: copyright Newtons, Leicester

Page 95 *top*: copyright Hulton Press Ltd

Windsor Castle was given its fashionably romantic attire
by Sir Jeffrey Wyatville in 1826

# PROLOGUE

TO MOST OF US perhaps history is still an assembly of dates. In the
mind these are bundled together into royal parcels, 'now stamped',
like Thomas Hardy's gold coins, 'with the image of good Queen Bess
and now with a Bloody Mary', and labelled, as they were in the
schoolroom, good or bad, prosperous or lean. But it is not necessary
to be an historian to appreciate that periods of achievement, particularly in the field of art, are not likely in fact to coincide with the
length of a particular monarch's reign. It is true that the architectural
styles which are today loosely known as 'Georgian', flourished and

developed principally between the ascent of George I to the throne in 1714 and the death of George IV in 1830, but most people would agree that architecturally speaking the Victorian age began before the young queen's accession, and it is certain that some of its most characteristic features had vanished before her death. Yet, absurd as dates are, a study of the period must begin and end somewhere. Shall it start in 1835, the year when John Nash died, 'the man who was the symbol of all the nineteenth century hated most about the eighteenth century'? Or should we go back to 1818, the year of the Brighton Pavilion and the Church Building Society? Or even further back, to 1760, to the Gothic of Strawberry Hill and the Greek antiquities of Stuart and Revett? Shall we end in 1882 with the building of the Law Courts—that last great Gothic monument of the Victorian age? Or do we end in 1896 with the death of William Morris? There is scarcely a year, it seems, which does not hold some significance for architecture.

In such circumstances it may be best to choose dates which are important for symbolic value rather than for actual events. It is suggested, then, that this study begins in 1832 and ends in 1890. Architecturally speaking, these dates are comparatively uneventful. Socially and politically, however, they are of tremendous significance. It is true that the passing of the Reform Bill was no bloody revolution—however often the Earl of Winchilsea might use that epithet. The new half-million voters were a steady and reliable group of men, and the powers of the landlords remained as unquestioned, the condition of the poor as infamous as before. But the implications of the Bill were more significant than its accomplishments. The first crack had appeared in the traditional rule of the aristocracy, and through it peered, stern, pebble-eyed and unwinking, the middle classes, who were to set their stamp so indelibly upon the whole century. The second crack—

this time defacing the structure of Victorian middle-class society—occurred in 1890, the year which ushered in a period so alert with new ideas it seemed as though the century was making a death-bed repentance for a lifetime of artistic confusion and dishonesty.

The last decade of the century—that period of bamboo, bicycles and Beerbohm—has always been credited with its own atmosphere and character. It has indeed its own biographer in Mr Holbrook Jackson. It was a period of tremendous social advances and great foolishness. Its personalities, Dreyfus and Lottie Collins, Beardsley and Thomas Lipton, Oscar Wilde and Marie Corelli, Poynter and Buller, Rhodes and Chamberlain, vary from the ridiculous to the tragic, but both they and the events in which they were concerned seem to belong to the Edwardian era, and have no part in our story.

If these dates then are accepted as reasonable, then the period which they encompass can be divided, so far as its architecture is concerned, into three definite epochs. Each has its own perceptible character and each is dominated aesthetically by a powerful personality whose ideas, it will be shown, were usually more inspiring than the architecture which expressed them. The first or Romantic epoch (1832–1845) is really the tail-end of the eighteenth century. The classic tradition is still strong and though Gothic is gaining ground it is as yet no more than a disguise, a fretted mask fixed insecurely upon a Greco-Roman face. The period is dominated by A. W. Pugin, and its architectural landmarks are the Houses of Parliament (1840–1850) and St George's Hall, Liverpool (1838–1854).

Over the second or Christian epoch (1845–1860) hangs a strong odour of ecclesiology. This is the period of increasing prosperity and increasing introversion. Its prophet is John Ruskin, its pedagogue the

11

Camden Society, its monuments All Saints, Margaret Street, and the Oxford Museum.

The third or Secular epoch (1860–1880) is almost concealed beneath its rich leathery skin of wealth and complacency. But beneath, all is movement. There is scepticism and unrest. William Morris is the spokesman for the new architectural ideas of this period, the Law Courts and The Red House Bayswater are two of its most important buildings.

The development of architecture in Epoch I is fairly straight-forward, for the stream is still running fresh and strong from the eighteenth century. In Epochs II and III it becomes more complicated. The stream is diverted into many twisting channels. It is joined by new tributaries, fed by new springs. There are short-cuts to be traced, ruthless and dogmatic scars across the landscape. Some of them become backwaters, others will later re-join the main stream. But by 1890, when our story ends, the surviving streams are re-uniting into the great shallow delta of Edwardianism.

So much for the general picture. In the following pages, a chapter has been devoted to each epoch in turn, and since architecture cannot be understood without some knowledge of the society it serves, an attempt has been made to weave the pattern of architectural development on to the general background of the time.

## 1832–1845

ALL PERIODS ARE THOSE of transition and contrast. The English gentleman who had been born in 1800 was no doubt aware of this, because even the most boisterous, free-mouthed and tyrannical of his

The Great Hall at Euston Station was designed to form a suitably
dramatic prelude to the adventure of travelling by rail

class was usually well read. But he might perhaps be excused for
thinking that the transition and contrasts of his own time were perhaps unduly swift and unpleasantly sharp.

Abroad, it was true, there was peace. After long years of effort, a
powerful totalitarian system had been destroyed by Great Britain and
her allies, and a profitable trade had been started at Hull in grinding
down the human bones shipped over from the many battlefields of
Europe. But the peace was an uneasy one. Already sparks of resur-
gence were visible among the timbers of the rickety structure erected

13

at the Congress of Vienna, while at home England was on the threshold of two revolutions, the mechanical revolution of organized science and the machine, and the social and financial revolution which was its accompaniment. The monarchy was derided, the Church comatose, the people restless. Control was passing from the aristocracy to the producers of goods. The chandeliers of Holland House were paling in the glare of the furnaces from the Midland industrial towns. Wordsworth, leaning on the parapet of Westminster Bridge, might well exclaim at the splendid vision of a wealthy city as it appeared to him that fine Sunday morning in 1802. But forty years later, Engels, the disciple of Karl Marx, looked over the parapet of Ducie Bridge upon a very different prospect. 'A narrow, coal-black, foul-smelling stream full of debris and refuse . . . disgusting, blackish-green slime pools . . . unendurable stench . . . the filth and offal from the courts on the left bank . . . houses black, smoky, crumbling, ancient, with broken panes and window-frames . . . the pauper burial-ground, the railway station, the workhouse. . . .'

Such conditions could be found in nearly every big city. London was noisy, dirty, undisciplined, a terrifying place at night—even to the new 'Peelers'. The tenements of the poor, jostling round the gates of the rich, were the breeding-grounds of vice and disease. The inhabitants lived by trades of unimaginable squalor, hunting the sewers for flotsam, or selling the excrement of dogs to the tanners of Battersea for a shilling a bucket. Every street had its quota of cripples, and cholera was so prevalent that the gentry would burn tar-barrels at their gates as a precaution. Even royalty was not immune, and a footman's sore throat led to the discovery of over 50 brimming cesspools beneath Windsor Castle itself.

Such conditions, while they were accepted as 'natural'—after all

Holywell station is designed in the Italian manner

were they not in accordance with the teachings of the fashionable economists of the day?—were dangerous to the person even if they were not disturbing to the conscience. So, while no immediate improvement followed the Reform Bill, a number of Royal Commissions were set up to investigate the more serious questions, Lord Shaftesbury began his crusade of social reform, and in 1842 Mr Chadwick published the famous report upon which is based most of our modern public health legislation.

The architect was confused and alarmed by this sinister and unfriendly background. Released from the shelter of the nobility, whence had previously come the bulk of his work, and not yet accepted by the new rulers of England either as lackey, teacher or friend, his position

15

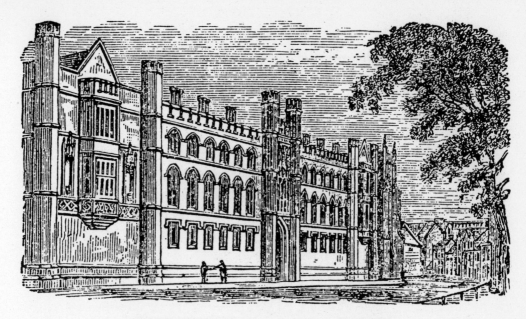

The Gothic front of Corpus College, Cambridge
is a veneer upon a Classical framework

was indeed a difficult one. It is true that his profession was by now reasonably well established. The pupilage system, aided by travel abroad, was accepted as the best training, the Institute of Architects had been granted in 1837 a Royal Charter, the fee of 5 per cent on the cost of the work was generally agreed to, and one of the first acts of King William had been to confer a knighthood upon John Soane. But despite these comforts, the relationship between the architect and the society he served remained unhealthy, even absurd. Sometimes he was little more than a 'modiste', dispensing taste from an inner sanctum in which he privately arranged and re-arranged his puppetry of styles. Sometimes he was an archaeologist, sometimes a preacher of morals. More often than not he was a reasonably competent artist as well, and this period does not lack its share of able designers. But architecture had become a private game which only those who knew

16

the 'dormitory talk' could play. In this game two languages were essential, one Greco-Roman, the other medieval. Though bilingualism was almost universal, each language had its particular specialists and of these the Greco-Roman company was by far the larger.

The publication in 1762 of the first volume of Stuart and Revett's *Athenian Antiquities* had injected the eighteenth-century dilettantism with a new spirit of scholarship. In the great country houses antiquarianism had become a craze, with Greek gradually replacing Roman as the favoured culture. The chief practitioners entrusted with the task of expressing this culture were Nash, Soane, Elmes, Cockerell and Barry.

John Nash (1752–1835) is so eminently an eighteenth-century character that he seems out of place in the story of Victorian architecture, and indeed most of his life's work was completed before our story begins. But his achievements, careless and theatrical as they appear to some scholars, had a tremendous influence upon Early Victorian building and particularly upon the vast speculative enterprises of the suburbs and provincial towns. The works of Foulston at Plymouth, of Papworth at Cheltenham, of Burton at Hastings, and of Robson at Newcastle, may be less famous than the terraces of Regent's Park, but their breadth of treatment is equally splendid and the visual pleasure they give is certainly no less intense.

Sir John Soane (1753–1837), one of the most distinguished and original architects in our history, breathed new life into the old classic motifs. He was no pedant and he was not afraid to handle them with freshness and daring. His architecture, taut, nervous, tensely balanced, shows that he had no rival in the art of controlling and moulding space and it is a tragedy that so little of his work survives—the old Bank of England having been mutilated by later additions, his Dulwich gallery

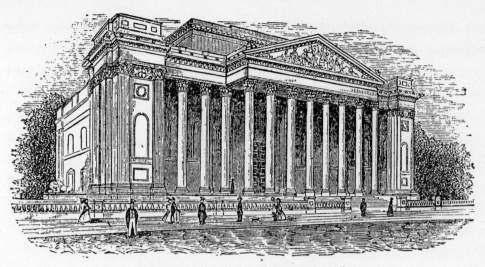

The Belgravian hand of George Basevi
lies heavy upon the Fitzwilliam Museum, Cambridge

by German bombs. Visitors to his house in Lincolns Inn Fields, now preserved as the Soane Museum, will, however, be rewarded by a dazzling display of his skill and imagination in the handling of a domestic interior.

Harvey Elmes (1813–1847) will always be remembered for St George's Hall, Liverpool, the noblest classical building of the century and described by Queen Victoria as 'one of the finest of modern buildings'. Elmes had won the competition for its design at the age of 25, but he died of consumption before its completion, and his work was conscientiously carried on by C. R. Cockerell (1788–1863), better known perhaps as a scholar and lecturer than as an architect. As a young man he had travelled widely in the Near East with an architect called Foster from Liverpool. They had many adventures, but Cockerell eventually went on alone, finding Foster perhaps lacking in serious application. 'In Crete,' Cockerell records, 'Foster found nothing of interest except numbers of pretty girls, some of whom were

18

so pressing he found it difficult to get away.' Cockerell built up a steady practice in banks and insurance offices which he treated with competence and dispatch, and he designed one reasonably distinguished building—the Taylor Institute at Oxford.

Sir Charles Barry (1795–1860), versatile, able and aristocratic, established in his designs for the Travellers' and Reform Clubs in Pall Mall an efficient and imposing formula for these buildings which was later to be much imitated but never surpassed. His major work, the Houses of Parliament, was carried out, superficially at least, in another language and will be described later.

Other notable designers in the Greco-Roman manner were William Wilkins (1778–1839), whose works include the National Gallery, University College, London, and St George's Hospital; Sir Robert Smirke (1781–1867), the designer of the British Museum with its splendid marching colonnade; Decimus Burton (1800–1881), designer of the Athenaeum, the Hyde Park Corner Screen and the Palm House at Kew; George Basevi (1794–1845), architect of Belgrave Square and the Fitzwilliam Museum; Sir William Tite (1798–1873), designer of the Royal Exchange and specialist in railway stations; David Mocatta (1806–1882), the designer of bridges and stations for the London Brighton & South Coast Railway; and Sir James Pennethorne (1801–1871), the pupil of Nash and architect of the ballroom at Buckingham Palace.

The motifs these men used and the rules to which in general they kept were still those most generally understood and employed throughout the country, in town and country alike. The speculative builder, from millionaire contractors like Thomas Cubitt and James Burton (father of Decimus) down to the smallest one-man business, worked, broadly speaking, in the language of pediment, cornice and sashbar. Gothic was as yet confined to the fashionable activities of the nobility, and to the traditional technique of the remote country craftsman. Towards the end of the eighteenth century the emotional qualities of Gothic had been exploited to the full under the stimulus of Walpole, Pope, Bentley and Thomas Gray. By 1800 this literary phase had assumed an even more Romantic character. Among the more advanced in thought, the middle ages had superseded classical times as the cultural ideal. Gothic sentiment was fashionable, and if the English gentleman's house was not his castle, it was no fault of his or of his architect. For this was the period of the *Waverley Novels*, the *Gentleman's Magazine*, the oriel and the battlement, of Ashridge, Abbotsford, Belvoir and Fonthill, and of those two Romantic works of scenery, the Houses of Parliament and New Court, St John's College, Cambridge. Even the Church began to yield to the fashionable clamour and 174 out of the 214 churches built under the Million Pounds Act, 1818, were in the Gothic style, though since Gothic was still vaguely associated with Popery the results were meagre, papery and thin. All the great classical masters, perhaps with the help of the pattern books now available, tried their hand at Gothic. Nash hated it. 'One window,' he said, practical as usual, 'costs more trouble than five houses ought to do.' Charles Barry was even more practical. When, after the great fire of 1834, it was decided to rebuild the Houses of Parliament in the Gothic style, he, as author of the winning design, had the good sense to call in a real Gothic enthusiast to help him with the task. This man was Augustus Welby Pugin (1812–1852), with whom he had previously collaborated at St Edward's School, Birmingham. Together they worked on the drawings while outside the storm of controversy raged between the protagonists of Classic and the supporters of Gothic. As it turned out, both sides won, for the building is a Classic

20

frame clothed in a Gothic skin, and it is now generally agreed that so far as the partnership was concerned, the former was provided by Barry, and the latter by Pugin. The Houses of Parliament, for all its aesthetic faults and technical blunders, is perhaps of all buildings of any period the most beloved by Englishmen. It has never failed to stir the imagination and affection of every succeeding generation, to such an extent that even today when we think of London we think nearly always of Barry and Pugin's building and not of St Paul's, the Abbey or Buckingham Palace. The Houses of Parliament was the last of the picturesque Gothic buildings and even before its completion it was rejected by the purists as 'late' and, following the fashionable biological fallacy, therefore decadent. From now on the Gothic style was to enter a sterner phase. Pilot in this changeover from Romance to Dogma was Pugin, son of a well-born French refugee, who had worked for Nash and published successful books of architectural drawings. He had had a strict upbringing, followed by a life of desperate industry. At 15 he was designing furniture for Windsor Castle and scenery for Covent Garden. By the time he was 22 he had been in prison for debt, had buried a wife and joined the Roman Catholic Church. At the age of 25 he published at his own expense *Contrasts*— 'a slim little book by a slim little man'—showing, in a series of contrasted drawings, how Gothic, and only Gothic, was the architectural answer to every problem. Gothic to him was a living art—not an exercise or a pastime. He derided the thoughtless application of Gothic ornament as a fashionable disguise. 'The man,' he wrote, 'who remains any length of time in a modern Gothic room and escapes without being wounded by some of its *minutiae* may consider himself to be extremely fortunate.' In 1841, he published *True Principles* in which he again expounded his faith in Gothic. 'There should be no features,' he wrote, 'about a building which are not necessary for convenience, construction or propriety. . . . All ornament should consist of enrichment of the essential construction of the building . . .' So far so good. But the fallacy was to come. Only in pointed architecture, said Pugin, could these principles be properly carried out. Even worse followed. Good buildings, he thought, could only be produced by good men, and since the only good buildings were Gothic ones, the

This drawing of the Albert Bridge, Saltash, shows how unafraid the engineers were of the strange forms created by structural needs

only good life was the medieval one and this in logic he was compelled to follow. In his house at Ramsgate he would don his velvet cloak, and work feverishly and alone at his drawings—'a clerk,' he said, 'I should kill him in a week!'—remote from the world outside which seemed so reluctant to accept his teaching.

Pugin was better at establishing principles, however questionable, than at carrying them out. His houses at Salisbury and Ramsgate, his church work at Birmingham and Derby, and even his fantastic outflow of decorative detail for the Houses of Parliament only dimly

22

reflect the vigour and inspiration of his writings, which were later to rouse even Gilbert Scott (in his own words) 'from his slumbers'. Cynical, meteoric, imaginative and hopelessly inconsistent, Pugin never knew in life the fame and honour he deserved. He died insane from overwork, on the same day as the Duke of Wellington, and so even in death his name was not remembered. But he had won his fight. Gothic was by now firmly established. It only had now to be argued which period of Gothic was the best.

So busy were the architects and critics in studying medieval architecture in search of the right answer to this that they missed perhaps the most important point of all. It was this. In medieval and Baroque times, new scientific discoveries had been reflected in contemporary art and architecture. This was no longer true. The contact of art and science was broken. 'Why,' cried Samuel Sidney, the author of *Railway Rides*, 'are our architects so inferior to our engineers?' To this cry there was only one answer. For the first time in history architects were not building honestly, nor making full use of the technical resources available to them. It is true they had been known to use cast iron—after all it had been sanctified by royal approval in the Brighton Pavilion—but usually in places where it didn't show, and nearly always without a true understanding of its properties. It was left to the engineers to exploit to the full the potentialities of this and other new materials. During the first third of the century, these men were transforming the face of England. The age of canal-building was over but the railway age had only just begun. By 1845 a network of railways covered a large proportion of England, a vast road improvement programme was under way, and the electric telegraph was in use. England, already the centre of world trade, became thus for the first time a united nation within her own shores, due largely to the

23

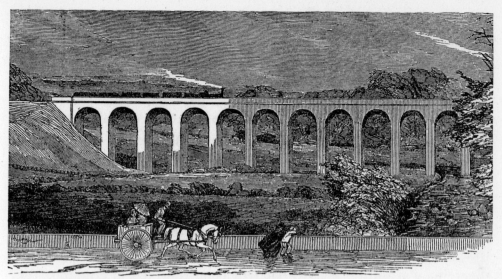

Ogwen Viaduct is one of the many simple but impressive brick structures
designed by the railway engineers

work of the handful of humbly born but great engineers of this
period. John Rennie, junior (1794–1874), the self-confident industrious
son of a famous father, foundation member of the Athenaeum and
builder of docks and bridges and the canal systems, who on his frequent trips abroad would comment so unfavourably upon the
'wretched waterworks' of Europe's great cities: Telford (1757–1834),
builder of the Menai Bridge and St Katharine's Dock: I. K. Bruneel
(1806–1859), son of another famous engineering family, and builder
of the Great Western Railway: Charles Fowler, designer of the huge
iron and glass markets of Hungerford and Covent Garden.

But, said the architects, as they glanced up from their scholarly
researches, none of this is *architecture*. How could it be? To start with,
none of the designers are gentlemen. And secondly, what *moral*
message was there in a tubular bridge? It was this question of a
building's morals which was to trouble architectural minds for the
next decade.

24

BY NOW THE EIGHTEENTH CENTURY was dead—driven finally underground by the advance of middle-class evangelicism. Traces appeared above the surface still—in a few great country houses, in the bawdy brutalities of the industrial slums, in the swaggering opportunism of England's idol, Lord Palmerston. But the mid-Victorian's pride in these relics of a former culture was limited to the sort of shamefaced pride a rake might feel in a skin-blemish denoting an ill-spent youth. For this was the age of self-discipline and good works. Goodness in fact was pursued almost as eagerly as prosperity, and the reigning sovereign was setting a good pace. Queen Victoria—'a little tit of 18', wrote Creevey, 'made all at once into a Queen', had already restored the monarchy to a place of honour and respect in the nation's heart. She had married in 1840, and though it was noted with misgiving that the royal couple had risen early on their honeymoon morning, they had already established a standard of family bliss and personal rectitude which was to set the note for the whole of mid-Victorian *Bourgeois* society, a note, it must be admitted, which was to sound a little false at times. It was not long before a whiff of cant had begun to invade the air. 'A typical congregation,' writes a chronicler of this period, 'is one which would be equally horrified at hearing Christianity doubted or at seeing it practised.' Religious faith was hardening into a code of puritanism. As early as 1837, a verger in St Paul's Cathedral had disconnected the bellows during an organ recital by Mendelssohn because, in his opinion, the fellow had gone on long enough, while a few years later *The Times* was remarking of a picture by Etty that some of the characters in it were exposing their persons in a way that called for the interference of the police. But the zeal for

Large roof spans like this one above a night-light factory
were among the problems facing Victorian architects and engineers

goodness had more valuable results than the provision of chained Bibles in railway station waiting rooms. 'Virtue,' wrote Newman, 'is the child of knowledge, vice of ignorance. Education, periodical literature, railroad travelling, ventilation and the art of life, when fully carried out, serve to make a population moral and happy.' There was evidence that the ingredients of this recipe were available in abundance. True the most serious maladies of town life had not been cured, but things were improving. The recommendations of Royal Commissions were beginning to take effect. The Factory Act was accompanied by other legislation designed for social reform. The writings of Dickens and Kingsley, the devoted angry zeal of Lord Shaftesbury, the humane sincerity of Prince Albert, were daily pricking the hide of complacency which was thickening over the Victorian character. At

26

times this complacency seemed almost justified, for who could doubt that England was on the threshold of a Golden Age? There had been of course riots in France and a terrible famine in Ireland—but what could you expect from such unreliable countries? The gold rushes in Australia and the Klondike showed of what Anglo-Saxon blood, however black the sheep in which it flowed, was capable. As for the Crimean War against Russia, nobody even knew what all that was about. Even Lord Raglan, the C.-in-C., habitually and absent-mindedly referred to the enemy as 'the Frenchies'—and anyway, like the Indian Mutiny which followed it, it was being dealt with by professionals and there was plenty else to occupy the mind at home. The building trade, for instance, was humming. Balmoral for the Queen and Saltaire for the factory workers were both begun in 1853; Wellington College, one of the new public schools, was completed in 1859—'a handsome edifice in the mixed style,' said *The Times*, 'which lends an air of animation to the bleak and inhospitable moor upon which it stands.' Every city and town was being extended with belts of villas for the swelling £2,000 a year class, while the working-classes were being admirably looked after by Mr Henry Roberts in model tenements, which still stand in Streatham Street, Bloomsbury. Even the lunatics were not forgotten and an alarming increase in their number noted in Surrey was being catered for by a new asylum at Woking. And to set the seal on the success of the age came the Great Exhibition in 1851. Conceived by Prince Albert as an opportunity of showing the artistic and industrial power of the civilized world, its realization owed much to Sir Henry Cole, a man of many interests and abilities, to whose later enthusiasm we owe the Victoria and Albert Museum and the Albert Hall. The usual competition for the building ended in the usual bickerings and indecision, but finally the design of

27

Crystal Palace interior
'We see a delicate network of lines without any clue by means of which we might judge
their distance from the eye, or the real size' (Lothar Bucher, 1851)

Joseph Paxton, one-time gardener of the Duke of Devonshire, was accepted, though it was irregularly submitted after the contest was closed. It was well known that Sir Henry Cole (known as 'Old King Cole of the Brompton Boilers'), like the Prince Consort, preferred engineers to architects. The Crystal Palace was the first large prefabricated building ever built. The design was planned round the largest sheet of glass then obtainable, four feet long, and the structural members were of standardized manufacture designed to be assembled on the site. In this way a building four times the size of St Peter's was erected in six months. The exhibition, like the exhibition building, was an unqualified success. Thousands attended the royal opening and gaped at Paxton's achievement—'a blazing arch of lucid glass,' wrote Tennyson, 'leaps like a fountain from the grass.' All persons admitted to the opening were commanded to appear *en grande toilette*, and the sight was said to rival the Coronation in splendour. It is interesting to note that the building encountered no opposition from the public, who appreciated its elegance and economy of structure without question. Not so the architects. Even Pugin, who was in charge of the medieval section, advised Paxton to stick to his greenhouses and leave architecture to the experts.

Paxton, however, who was to become Sir Joseph, was a man of determination as well as of invention and was soon unabashedly designing a twelve-mile glazed arcade to encircle London.

Nobody seemed to notice the sharp contrast between the clean direct building and the cargo of over-decorated rubbish which it housed. This conflict between Art and Industry was paralleled by the conflict arising between Science and Faith. The Church itself was forced to emerge from its torpor and to plunge immediately into a fog of argument which was to prove both confusing and dangerous. At Oxford, Newman and his followers were delving into seventeenth-century theology, arguing over ritual, drifting farther along the road to Rome. Members of the clergy were disquieted or thrilled by this new fashion for taking Christianity seriously. An indecisive cleric called Sibthorpe changed his faith to Rome, back to the Church of England and then over to Rome again. At Cambridge, the Cambridge Camden Society stood like a piece of granite in this conflict of opposing tides. The rules it drew up for church building were decided, and so ruthlessly imposed that from 1845 onwards church architecture became an exact science, and woebetide the architect whose morals did not pass the Society's approval or who forgot, after his appointment, to

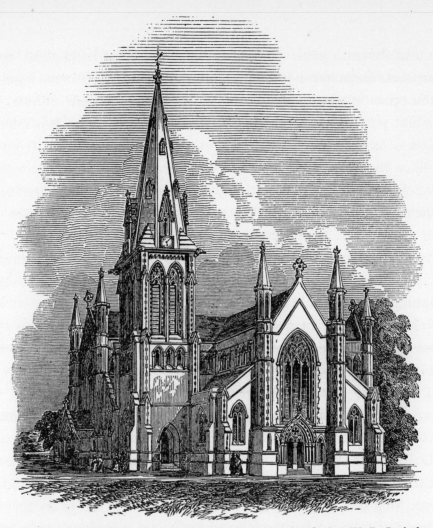

This church at Highbury is an uncompromising example of what W. R. Lethaby used to call the 'hard school' of Gothic revivalism

follow the instructions prepared for his benefit. So far as style was concerned, the Camden Society followed again the biological fallacy which insists that a style is born, matures and decays, and that because the middle period is the most vigorous it is therefore the best. Middle Pointed was therefore chosen as the officially approved style.

In William Butterfield (1814–1900) the Society found an architect after its own heart. This stern, shy, uncompromising man had no interest in life except that of church building and a surprising weakness for Regency furniture. His morals were beyond question, his architecture always trustworthy if usually ugly. Butterfield believed in the discipline of geometry and the value of primary colours for enrichment. He liked to use only the hardest and most durable of materials, and if paint could not be trusted to keep its colour then the more permanent tints of coloured bricks and tiles would have to be used. He had no use for the softening effects of Nature, and if he found a creeper presuming to encroach upon one of his buildings, he would cut it down, and cover the roots with concrete. His most famous buildings, All Saints, Margaret Street (1849–1859), St Albans, Holborn (1860–1863) and Keble (1870), have been compared unfavourably with pieces of linoleum, and of their forceful angularity and harsh colouring there can perhaps be no question. But it is possible to respect the awkward vigour of an architecture which, in its rejection of the suave and mellow, so faithfully reflects the rigid standards and unyielding faith of its creator.

In his use of coloured brick patterns, Butterfield was anticipating the teaching of John Ruskin (1819–1900), who for the whole of this period was the prophet and dictator of aesthetic tastes. Ruskin was born of strict and wealthy parents who hoped that he would become a Bishop. His early training in the Bible, of which he knew whole sections by heart, was to infect his style in later years with a rolling rhetoric, which prevents perhaps the thirty-five volumes he produced being so widely read as they deserve. Like Pugin, he became obsessed with the problem of architecture and morals, and much of his teaching, wittingly or not, reflected the brilliance of Pugin's mind. But though *Seven Lamps of Architecture* only followed a very few

The Victorian ideal of good works coupled with mechanical progress is well illustrated in this picture of the Freemasons' School, Battersea Rise

years after Pugin's *True Principles*, Ruskin would never admit that he owed anything to the latter. Ruskin was engaged on the task of placing the Protestant Church upon a firm, respectable basis and there was a whiff of incense about Pugin which debarred him from even the most indirect share in the task. 'I owe nothing to Pugin,' he wrote, '. . . he is only the smallest possible of conceivable architects.' And again, 'I have not felt the smallest possible interest in his opinions.' He shared, however, many of Pugin's characteristics—the burning enthusiasm and sensibility, the frequent inconsistencies and boundless assurance. Though rich, Ruskin was never idle, and he was genuinely disturbed by the sufferings and stupidity of society. Like William Morris, to whom he handed his prophet's cloak, he found eventually that art could not put these errors right without social reform, and he unhesitatingly switched his energies to this new

32

activity. His experiments in Hinksey Road and the Paddington tea-shop have often been dismissed as foolish dilettantism, but few men have worked harder and with more sincerity for what they believed to be right. His influence on contemporary artistic thought was over-whelming. When he decided that Gothic was suitable for secular as well as for church building, and that North Italian Gothic was superior to the French or English version, his views were instantly obeyed. At his door, alas, must be laid the stumpy column, the striped brickwork and multi-coloured window arches which distin-guish the bulk of the buildings of this era, and which were to persist in unfashionable areas right into the twentieth century. To him the classic orders meant paganism. 'Whatever has any connection with the five orders,' he wrote, 'whatever is in any way Grecized or Roman-ized—that we are to endure no more.' And again 'The glory of Gothic is that it will do *anything*.' He was taken at his word. Ruskin was aware that many of the results from his teaching were ugly and mis-shapen and this caused him distress. 'There is scarcely a public-house,' he wrote sadly in 1872, 'but sells its gin and bitters under pseudo-Venetian capitals.' But with those who tried to apply his doc-trines to industrial buildings he had no patience. 'Architecture,' he wrote, 'is something different from a rat-hole, a wasp's nest or a railway station.' A factory could not, in his opinion, be anything but hideous. He could see no merit in the Crystal Palace. But for all his assertiveness and inconsistency—as a young man he defended Turner against almost the same charges that he was later himself to hurl at Whistler—he had the power of imparting enthusiasm, and he kept alive the visual awareness which is so vital an ingredient of a flourish-ing art, and which since his death has almost ceased to exist.

If Ruskin succeeded with his pen in making Gothic more widely popular, Sir Gilbert Scott (1811–1878) can be said to have done the same with his tee-square. Scott, described by Mr Goodhart-Rendel as 'a man of talents other than architecture . . . and full of ideas, few of them his own', was an industrious, devout and pertinacious architect who did too much work for any of it to be really good. Many anecdotes are told of his fantastic practice which was based on a firm foundation of Poor Law institutions and church restoration, and included town halls, public institutions and the Albert Memorial (described by the *Telegraph* as 'assuredly the most consummate and elegant piece of elegant art which modern genius has produced'). It was said that he could take a ticket to any railway station in the country and be sure of being within easy reach of one of his jobs. It was said that once, on passing a new church, he asked who the architect was and was told that it was his own work. True or not, such stories indicate the place Gilbert Scott held in the architectural field of the time and, for all his faults, it is certain he could not have held it for so long if he had been entirely without skill or ability. Like many second-rate and successful architects, he was a frequent winner of competitions and an expert at organizing indignation if, through some oversight, his designs were not placed first. But in Lord Palmerston, who disliked architects as much as he disliked Gothic, he met his match. Scott, who had been appointed by the Government previously in power to design the new Foreign Office in Whitehall, had of course produced a Gothic design. Lord Palmerston, however, would have none of it. Nor would he accept Scott's second scheme, a Byzantine compromise which his Lordship described as a 'regular mongrel'. Five years elapsed after the first scheme before Scott capitulated and produced a set of façades in the Italian manner. But this defeat in Whitehall was followed by a Gothic victory in the

34

Euston Road, where Sir Gilbert was given a free hand with St Pancras Station, which, he used to say, was 'possibly too good for its purpose'. Other notable buildings by this very typical Victorian architect are St Giles, Camberwell (1844), St Nicholas, Hamburg (1844), Preston Town Hall (1852) and Glasgow University (1872).

Assisting Butterfield, Ruskin and Scott in the task of ensuring the supremacy of Gothic during the 'fifties were Pearson, Carpenter, Street, Burges, Bodley, Brandon and Deane.

J. L. Pearson (1817–1897) designed a number of suburban churches in London, the most famous of which is St Augustine's, Kilburn, the most brilliantly successful St John's, Red Lion Square, badly damaged by bombing. R. C. Carpenter was the architect of Lancing College Chapel and of St Paul's, Brighton, while G. E. Street (1824–1881), the industrious, choir-singing pupil of Scott and later the idol of all young architects, was busy on All Saints, Clifton. In 1853, William Burges (1827–1881) had won, with Clutton, the important international competition for Lille Cathedral—never in fact to be built—and had also published a best-selling sketchbook of thirteenth-century Gothic details. His works include Cardiff Castle and Harrow School speech room. G. F. Bodley (1827-1907), who built many churches all over the country, was the architect of Washington Cathedral, R. Brandon (1817–1877) designed the famous Catholic Apostolic Church in Gordon Square, while T. N. Deane (1828–1899), partner of Woodward, was responsible for Meadow Buildings, Christchurch, and the Oxford Museum.

Gothic, once Romantic, then Christian, was now respectable, universal, the style 'as worn'. It seemed unassailable, but in fact its days were numbered.

35

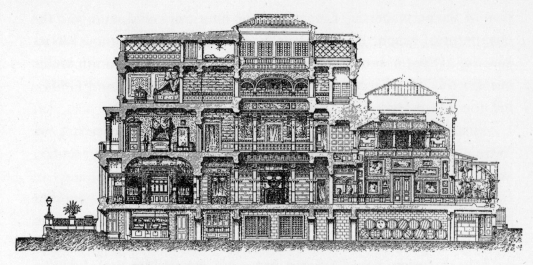

This section through the Vanderbilt House, New York,
exposes a Victorian interior as rich and heavy as plum cake

## 1860-1890

THE NEXT THIRTY YEARS of the nineteenth century epitomize every-
thing that most people think of when they use the adjective 'Victorian'.
It was, admittedly, an unattractive and over-stuffed period, dominated by a smug, narrow and self-reliant middle-class which was fully
absorbed in the task of accumulating wealth. Poverty was despised
and dreaded but seldom pitied, and society was built upon an un-
questioning faith in the sanctity of the Family and the Home. Never
perhaps in any country and at any time has the Home meant so much
as it did to the Victorians of the 'sixties. Home meant property—
'all the meaningless impedimenta poured from the cornucopia of
Free Trade'—and property was more important even than people,
theft more severely punished than assault.

The highly prized Victorian home was built upon the triple foundation of the permanence of marriage, the inferiority of woman and the cheapness of labour. Such a foundation appears frail enough today, but eighty years ago it seemed unshakable, and to the faith which sustained it the stuccoed acres of Bayswater, Kensington and Pimlico are the monument. The architects of these endless grey façades, Mr Clough Williams-Ellis has suggested, must have had one sense lacking. Were they perhaps, he asks, deaf? And what were they like inside, these huge mansions, six, seven or eight storeys high, in the days of their glory when there were servants to answer the rows of bells in the cavernous basements, and the landings were uncluttered with kitchenettes and apple-green matchboarding? Let's take a look and see.

'The Victorian home,' writes Mr Alan Bott, 'like the Victorian female body, was well covered, and like the Victorian female mind, filled to overflowing with superfluities . . . wherever a drapery could be draped, there it hung . . . dark, dull and expensive wallpapers . . . solid mahogany in the dining-room, rioting fancy in the drawing-room. Clocks, vases, embroidered stools, firescreens, what-nots, fancy brackets, wardrobes, toilet glasses, washstands, towel rails and pedestal cupboards. Every article stamped and carved and twisted with ornament, a machine-made imitation of the furnishings of the great feudal palaces which every Victorian householder set out to re-create within the confines of his own walls and the limitations of his pocket.' Embedded within this rich dark interior, 'like an earwig in the heart of a great crimson dahlia', was the master of the house, surrounded by his family, his servants, and his possessions.

The Victorian's delight in property, as epitomized in that personal museum, his home, is not merely a symptom of infantilism. It is a feature of society to be found always in times of unrest and changing values. For the point about the Victorian 'security' of the 'sixties was

37

that it was merely a façade, elaborate and finely modelled perhaps, richly decked and painted too, but fragile and treacherous as stucco. Already faint cracks indicated the shakiness of the structure beneath the covering. Religious faith was being ceaselessly undermined, the working classes no longer knew their place. *The Origin of Species* had been published in 1859; there was a Roman Catholic Archbishop enthroned in London; Girton College for lady undergraduates had been opened only two miles from Cambridge; Karl Marx, the one-time special constable of Camberwell, was uttering his fiery warnings—('How I wish,' said his mother, fretfully, 'Karl would make some capital instead of writing about it'). Worse still, Trades Unions had appeared. 'You have heard, no doubt,' Dr Arnold had written in 1839 to a friend, 'of Trades Unions. A fearful engine of mischief, ready to riot and assassinate.' 'I would rather live under a Bey of Algiers,' had said Cobden, 'than under a Trades Committee.' But here they were, legalized in 1875, growing fast, another milestone on the road from Peterloo and Tolpuddle to Transport House. But even the Trades Unions could cause little more than a faint chill of doubt to blow through the hot-house of material prosperity, with its riotous display of pompous vulgar blooms.

Leader in the revolt against the ugly commercialism of his time was William Morris (1834–1896). Like Ruskin, he was born of wealthy parents and intended for the Church. Like Ruskin too, he approached social reform through the study and practice of art. At Marlborough, then in so bad a state that one term there was an open rebellion among the boys, he was more interested in old churches than in organized games. Soon after he had reached Oxford (at the next desk in the examination room sat a boy who was to become his lifelong friend, Edward Burne-Jones) he had decided that building churches was more fun

38

than preaching in them, and that for him, for Burne-Jones and their intimate friends as well, happiness was to lie in a social and not in a monastic brotherhood. At this time Street was living and working in Oxford and though they did not meet, there is no doubt that his influence over Morris was a powerful one. So much so that when Morris decided to become an architect, he entered Street's office, where he found working another lifelong friend to be, Philip Webb. In the next few years his life followed conventional student lines. He wrote poetry. He practised painting. He grew a beard. He was a disciple of the current *avant-garde*, the pre-Raphaelites. Under the influence of Rossetti, he forsook architecture for painting and together with their friends they undertook the tempera painting of the Oxford Union frescoes. During this work, according to Mr Dudley Harbron, a pot of paint fell from a scaffold at the foot of a distinguished visitor. 'O tempora,' he sighed, stepping over the sludgy mess. 'O Mores.' In 1859 Morris married, and commissioned Philip Webb to build him a house. It was to prove a turning-point in the history of domestic architecture. At this time stucco, stone and slate were still supreme. The Red House at Bexley was, as its name implies, built of brick, and was treated as informally and directly as if it had been a Kentish farmhouse. It was L-shaped and possessed a high-pitched, red-tiled roof. Morris was determined to make the living room the most beautiful room in England. But here was the difficulty. There appeared to be nothing on the market in the way of textiles, furniture or pottery that was not vulgar or ugly to look at. The solution was clear. He and his friends would have to design and make them. Morris & Company was formed with this object, and they were soon busy on church decoration, commissioned by Street and Bodley. In addition to stained glass, metalwork, murals and furniture,

39

the firm undertook weaving and glass design and of course the famous wallpapers. The Morris family moved back to London and thence to Kelmscott which was to be their home for twenty-five years. To begin with, Rossetti shared the house with them, but he was ill-at-ease in the tiny hamlet set among the flat Oxfordshire meadows—'the doziest bunch of beehives you ever saw,' he called it—and he returned to London a few years before the estrangement between Morris and himself became complete. Morris soon realized that the sort of battle against commercialization which he and his friends were fighting was in vain. He believed that mechanization was the root of evil, and that artistic integrity could only be based on handcraft, and the love of the individual for his own work. But the products of Morris & Co. were bought only by the rich. He saw that social reform must come first. 'I do not want Art for a few,' he wrote, 'any more than I want education for a few, or freedom for a few . . . rather than the wheat rot in the miser's granary, I would that the earth had it, that it might yet have a chance to quicken in the dark.' And again, 'Let Art go, it will rise again whatever else lies there.' He plunged into the Socialist League, and worked ceaselessly for the cause. He died at the age of 63, his powerful physique worn out by a great and useful life, to which his poems, his pioneer work for the Arts and Crafts movement and, above all, his achievements in the field of design are a lasting memorial.

The Red House was not immediately recognized as the landmark in architectural history which it later became. It did not escape the notice of the malicious that the site was originally called Hogs Hole, and to the Gothicists it seemed as if Webb had dropped a brick at Bexley. But it was the first of a cartload. The Law Courts, the competition for which was won by Street in 1868, was the last great secular building in nineteenth-century Gothic, and was the target of much criticism when completed. A renaissance was in the air. By 1880 the 'Queen Anne' style—Burges called it 'negro language'—was established. 'Men and women,' wrote Max Beerbohm, 'hurled their mahogany into the street.'

This revolution from stone to brick and from lancet to sashbar was partly due to the influence of contemporary aesthetic movements and to the teachings of Webb and Morris, but principally perhaps to the buildings of J. J. Stevenson and Norman Shaw. J. J. Stevenson (1832–1908) was a Scotsman. He trained under Gilbert Scott, and was a friend of William Morris. He specialized in domestic work, and built many houses in London, including his most famous work, 'The Red House'—the second time this challenging name was used—which, said a contemporary critic, 'altered the whole character of London's street architecture'. The interior of this Bayswater house, which he built for himself, was designed by his friend Bodley—'After all,' he said, 'a man can't sit and look at his work all day.' Stevenson later joined E. R. Robson (1835–1917), architect to the London School Board, and designed, too, the public rooms of several Orient liners.

The influence of Norman Shaw (1831–1912) upon his contemporaries was perhaps even more overwhelming. 'There is something in Norman Shaw,' wrote his classics master in a school report, 'but it is certainly not Greek.' Not architecture either, say Shaw's critics, as they watch his steady progress downhill into the stony deserts of Edwardian Baroque. Such judgment is unfair to this architect's very considerable achievements. By entering Street's office as a pupil in 1858, he showed that as a youth he was an enthusiast for the fashionable Gothic, but fourteen years later he was building huge country houses in the romantic style which was to become the trademark of his early manner—barge-boarded, half-timbered, elaborately composed. In 1872 he

41

dared to introduce red brick into the heart of the City. New Zealand Chambers, with its ornamental plasterwork and arched three-light windows—a favourite Shaw motif—was to be copied all over the country for generations. In 1876 he began work with E. J. May and M. B. Adams in the model suburb of Bedford Park, near Hammersmith. This community was designed on the neighbourhood principle with its own shops, church and public-house, and was one of the earliest and most visually successful experiments of the garden city movement. 'Here trees are green,' wrote a contemporary poet, 'and bricks are red,

And clean the face of man.

We'll build our houses here he said,

In style of good Queen Anne.'

These romantically composed villas of Bedford Park, with their abundance of brick cornices, white painted balconies—'uncommon 'andy' commented a contemporary crook—and elaborate chimneys have not lost their charm and pleasant rusticity. They were followed by 170 Queen's Gate and Swan House, Cheyne Walk—two typical town houses in the soft Queen Anne style which Shaw by now had made peculiarly his own. By now he had forsaken Gothic completely. 'It is like a cut flower,' he said, 'pretty to look at, but fading away before your eyes.' Nobody could say that of his new buildings, the Royal Geographical Society building, Albert Hall Mansions, the houses in Melbury Road and Queen's Gate, and New Scotland Yard, built of Dartmoor granite and Portland stone. They stand today as solid, red, romantic, and brilliantly assured, as the day they were built. This brilliance, sadly dimmed in much of Shaw's later work, was carried on by his pupils, Prior, Newton, Macartney and Lethaby, the last for ten years his chief assistant. These men shared Pugin's enthusiasm for

42

sound materials and Morris's belief in honest construction and the delight of craftsmen in their work. By the time they were building, the battle was over. The first Town Hall in the new style had been built at Leicester in 1874–1876. E. R. Robson had adopted Queen Anne for those splendid schools of his and Stevenson's which still ride like ships above the crumpled roofs of suburban London. Queen Anne had become officially approved, and it was never again entirely to relinquish its grip upon the affections of the English people.

Not every architect of the 'sixties was won over so easily. Many of them, led by Sir Ernest George, were struggling with terra-cotta and with sketch-books full of details from Ghent and Amsterdam. Others were trying to stretch the Renaissance façade of an Italian villa or a French chateau over the carcase of an office block or a railway hotel. Ingenious attempts to solve this apparently hopeless task can be seen in Charing Cross Station by E. M. Barry (1830–1880), in Woolland's shop and the Holborn Viaduct Hotel, both by H. L. Florence (1842–1916), and in the Admiralty Buildings, Whitehall, by the north-country firm of the Leeming Brothers. There were even a few eclectics who pursued their own way—E. W. Godwin (1833–1886), designer of Northampton Town Hall, and more famous perhaps as one of Ellen Terry's lovers than as an architect, but deserving of a place if only because he was Whistler's architect, and because Max Beerbohm called him 'superb': Thomas 'Victorian' Harris, the bearded admirer of Paxton and the iron age, so much more conventional with his tee-square than with his pen: Alexander Thomson (1817–1875), the Egypto-Greek stylist of Glasgow, and Captain Fowke (1823–1865), the designer of the Albert Hall: Mr John T. Emmett, who wrote so scathingly about St Pancras Station that the porters ought to be dressed as javelin men and the station-master as Garter King of

43

Spalding station is an example of the informal domestic style
so popular for country railway stations

Arms. There were others again more pedestrian perhaps in imagination, but more prosperous in their practices: George Aitchison, Lord Leighton's architect, who successfully combined the posts of Professor of Architecture at the Royal Academy School and district surveyor of Tooting: Alfred Waterhouse (1830–1905), architect of the Prudential Assurance Building, Holborn, Manchester Town Hall, and the Metropole Hotel, Brighton, who carried the spluttering torch of Gothic and whose smile was said to be worth ten thousand a year to him: H. A. Darbishire, architect to the Peabody Trust, and designer of so many conscientious and depressing attempts to improve the living quarters of the poor: Aston Webb, who used to say that the plan of a house should contain an element of mystery and practised so unmercifully what he preached. But already we are in a later age, the period of electric light and labour exchanges, Home Rule and the Halfpenny Press, Art Nouveau and the Inner Circle, Imperialism and the beginnings of Socialism. The pace was quickening as the century went spinning to its close. The Victorian age was dead, ten years before the sovereign died whose name it bore.

# EPILOGUE

ARCHITECTURE, WE ARE often reminded, reflects the society and times for which it is built. The Victorian era was confused, romantic, packed with incident. No one could say that the same qualities are not abundantly displayed in Victorian architecture. The conflict between science and faith, between commercialism and social reform, between art and artiness, is written as clearly in stone and terra-cotta as it is in the pages of the history books, and no clearer indication of the individualism of the nineteenth century could be given than that given by its astonishing parade of highly individual buildings. The number of great personalities in all branches of achievement who were thrown up by the Victorian age has probably no parallel since the most brilliant days of the Renaissance. It is not just distance and the dimness of time which make men like Tennyson and Darwin, Gladstone and Shaftesbury, Disraeli and Dickens, loom like giants upon the horizon. But while their important positions in English history are reasonably assured, less than justice perhaps has been done to the great Victorian architects. (Not one, for instance, is included in the two volumes of

45

*The Great Victorians* by J. C. and Barbara Hammond.) Yet men like Soane and Barry, Pugin and Butterfield, Street and Shaw, are men of considerable stature even apart from the profession in which they were all so distinguished, and what more typical example of Victorian success could you find than Sir Gilbert Scott? The fertility of mind shown by these men and their colleagues was only equalled by their industry. The good old days so wistfully spoken of today were not days of leisure, whatever were their other alleged advantages. The hours in the elder Pugin's drawing office were 6 a.m. to 8 p.m. Young Pugin had been known to produce within fifteen minutes two completely different designs for a stained glass window. Charles Barry rose long before six and worked usually until midnight; and Soane's working day often exceeded twelve hours. Street was accustomed to deal with all his correspondence before breakfast, and after winning the Law Courts competition he spent two weeks on the Continent, drawing by day and travelling by night, never sitting down, it was said, except to eat or sleep. Norman Shaw, his biographer records, designed the whole of the vast palace of 'Cragside' while his fellow-visitors were out for a day's shooting. Nor was such industry considered exceptional; it was indeed thrust upon the architect by the speed-up of industry. He was working throughout a boom which was to last sixty years or more, and at a time when improved communications and advances in techniques were daily heaping the culture and produce of the civilized world at his feet. In this flood of new materials and new influences the Victorian architect was buoyed up by his boundless self-confidence in the rightness of what he was doing. And if he faltered in the buffeting of conflicting tides, there was always a life-guard on duty to help him out, Mr Pugin perhaps, or, more likely still, Mr Ruskin.

Inevitably, architecture conceived at such a time became paper architecture, divorced from honest building and direct design. The Victorians expected every building, like every painting, to tell a story, and preferably to point a moral as well. The Victorian architect was a man of his own period, and responded to this demand with a will, borrowing motifs from every country and period at his command. Flemish and Hindoo, Moorish and Venetian, Spanish, Gothic and Greek, the styles of East and West, new and old, are paraded by in all their panoply of texture and colour, marching and counter-marching into a kaleidoscope of patterns, like gaily caparisoned troops in some monster tattoo. But for all their changing complexity, the patterns are disciplined and firmly shaped. The men in command of these wheeling armies knew what they wanted, and manoeuvred their units with self-confidence. Only occasionally a Philip Webb, a John Emmett, or a Thomas Harris would fall out of step and wander off, deaf to the rhythm of the herd. Today we may laugh at the well-meant and self-assured play-acting of the Victorian-architect, just as we may regret that during the nineteenth century the history of architecture is little more than the assembled biographies of nineteenth-century architects. But before we dismiss that architecture as just a pageantry of over-durable problem pictures, 'as unpleasant, snobbish and well intended as grocer's port', let us not forget in comparison the uncertain and trivial architecture of our own time. Victorian architecture was possibly founded on confused values, but Pugin, Ruskin and Morris, as well as the architects who followed them, were right in their main thesis, that good architecture can only flourish in a good society. Most of contemporary architecture is based on money values which is another way of saying no values at all. We may laugh, too, at the artistic domination exercised by Ruskin, and indeed it was in many ways unhealthy and ridiculous. But before we condemn his inconsistency and fallible judgment, let us not forget the flaming enthusiasm and passionate sensibility which enabled him, and Morris and Pugin, too, to inspire the minds of so many of their brother artists and architects, and which even today is powerful enough to cast beams of searching brightness into the cold half-light of our own age.

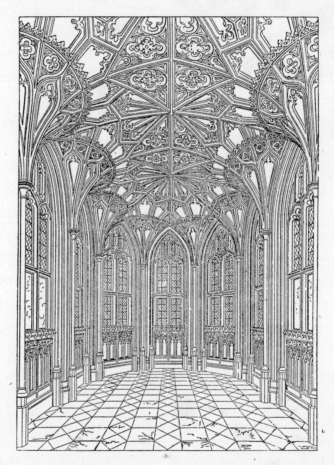

Chantry Chapel in the old St Stephen's Cloister,
now destroyed (From Brayley and Britton's *Westminster*, 1836)

The Houses of Parliament (1836–1860)
owes to Charles Barry the
simple symmetry of its
plan and grouping, and to
Augustus Pugin the
fretted elaboration of its detail

D

The scrupulous Gothic dress provided by Pugin
for the Houses of Parliament was already unfashionable
by the year of its completion (1860)

Kensal Green cemetery (1838)

The Naval Victualling Yard at Plymouth (designed by John Rennie)

Both are sturdy examples of the Greek Revival
which was given an added impetus by the
arrival here in 1801 of the Elgin Marbles

51

New Court, St John's College, Cambridge (1827), one of the
most romantic pieces of Gothic scenery of the 19th century, was designed by
Thomas Rickman (1776–1841), a Quaker turned Irvingite, a collector of toy soldiers
and the inventor of the nomenclature for the periods of the Gothic style

The Lower Market, Exeter, was built in 1835
to the design of the market specialist Charles Fowler

*Opposite, lower:* St Martin's School, Endell Street,
was designed by the unconventional James Wild

The porch of the parish church of Wilton,
unexpectedly designed (1843–4) in the Italian manner
by Wyatt and Brandon

It is said that the design of the interior of St George's Hall, Liverpool (1839–54), was based by the architect Harvey Elmes upon the tepidarium of the Baths of Caracalla

The fact that the Reform Club, Pall Mall (1837),
by Charles Barry, was inspired by the Farnese Palace, Rome,
does not prevent it from being a most distinguished building
in its own right.
The library furniture (*opposite, top*)
and the library of the Travellers' Club (1830) (*opposite, below*),
both by the same architect,
exhibit his equal mastery of detail
and of the formal interior

56

By 1838, when John Robertson remodelled this cottage
at Edensor, Derbyshire, the picturesque style
was beginning to pass under the relentless discipline
of antiquarianism

This simple house at Ramsgate
was built by Pugin in 1841
for his own occupation

60

The cast-iron column had been used as early as 1780
in the early English cotton mills.
In the riding school at Welbeck Abbey
it is used in conjunction with arched iron trusses
to solve a difficult vaulting problem

The Palm House at Kew (*opposite*), designed by Decimus Burton in 1844,
was not the first large iron-and-glass structure to be built.
Ten years earlier Rouhault, a Frenchman, had built a similar conservatory
in the Botanical Gardens, Paris,
and in 1837 Paxton was building huge greenhouses
to protect the tropical plants at Chatsworth

61

Among the new technical problems of the age were the great public markets. The Floral Hall, Covent Garden, designed by E. M. Barry, is one of the most elegant of these

*Above:* Cast-iron columns and wrought-iron ribs were used by I. K. Brunel and M. D. Wyatt to leap the 100 ft. span of Paddington Station (1855)

*Opposite:* In the Oxford Museum (1855–60) the architects Messrs Deane & Woodward were encouraged by Mr Ruskin to disguise the iron and glass structure within Gothic forms. It is interesting to compare this building with Labrouste's National Library built in Paris at the same time and of similar materials

63

A large number of town halls were built throughout England after The Municipal Corporation Act. Here are two typical examples in the fashionable manners, at Halifax (1862) by Sir Charles Barry and at Northampton (1864) by E. W. Godwin

A variety of architectural periods
is evoked in a typically 19th-century manner
by these buildings at the east end of Victoria Street, London

*Opposite:* two Victorian church spires compared.
On the left St Paul's, Brighton, designed by R. H. and R. C. Carpenter;
on the right, All Saints', Margaret Street, by William Butterfield

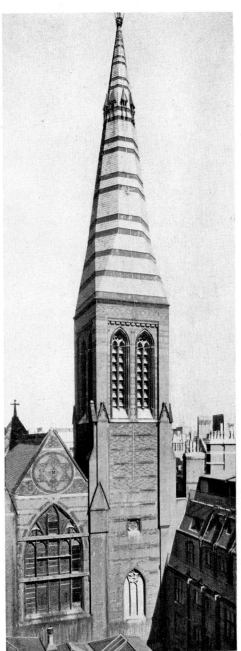

The stiff multi-coloured interior of All Saints', Margaret Street (1844–59),
is an excellent example of Butterfield's rigorous style

Edmund Scott shows a mastery of scale
in his interior of St Bartholomew's, Brighton (1875)

These model dwellings were built (1844–7) in Streatham Street, Bloomsbury,
to the designs of Henry Roberts, the pioneer architect of working-class housing

There was no bathroom in the
Red House, Bexley,
designed in 1859 for William Morris
by Philip Webb

A detail of the interior

Although by now Venetian or Gothic were the really fashionable domestic styles,
a clumsy version of Classic still survived in London
where the speculative builder was covering the stuccoed acres of Pimlico and Bayswater
with terrace houses for the newly rich middle classes

73

The Albert Memorial (1872) is perhaps the most famous and the most ridiculed structure of the Victorian age. It was designed by Sir Gilbert Scott, and Queen Victoria loved it.

The superbly confident piece of Victorian Gothic opposite is the Grand Staircase of the Town Hall, Manchester, designed (1868) by Alfred Waterhouse,
the architect of the Natural History Museum and Prudential Assurance Building in London

The Chamberlain Monument and Corporation Street, both in Birmingham, are fine examples of the commercial Gothic of the 'sixties

The Victorian restaurant was as solid, reliable
and pretentious as the Victorian meal.
The interior (*above*) is of Simpson's in the Strand,
the exterior (*opposite*) is of the Florence Restaurant in Beak Street

Industrial buildings are among the finest monuments of the Victorian age.
The warehouse in Lisson Grove (*above*) was designed (1874) by the eccentric Thomas Harris.
Calvert's Buildings is a Ruskinian warehouse in Southwark Street

This school in Whitfield Street is one of those stylistically advanced buildings designed for the London School Board by E. R. Robson and his associates

The Law Courts (1868–74), designed by G. E. Street after the settlement of a competition dispute, was the last great monument of the Gothic Revival

One of the doorways in this romantic but inconvenient building

Balmoral Castle,
designed in the 'fifties
by William Smith of
Aberdeen, was
described by
Queen Victoria as
'my dear Albert's *own*
creation, own work,
own building,
own laying-out'.
Its influence upon
'Allanbank',
Camden Road
(*at left*), designed in
1863 by Herbert Hodge,
is noticeable

*Opposite :*
Kelham Hall, Notts,
is an ambitious essay
in country-house Gothic
by Sir Gilbert Scott

85

Whether Gothic or Classic in inspiration
the Victorian interior always gave value for money.
The vaulted library (*opposite*) is from Kelham Hall,
the modelled dome (*above*) from Covent Garden (1859) by E. M. Barry

The hall of Coleherne Court, Kensington,
exhibits all the rich confusion of the typical Victorian home.
You can almost hear the dressing-gong
booming up the Turkey-carpeted staircase

Cadogan Square is built in the Flemish Renaissance manner
so popular in the 'eighties.
Characteristics of this style, of which Sir Ernest George was the principal exponent,
are a fondness for asymmetry and vertical emphasis,
and a preference for bow windows and gables
carried out in bright red brick enriched with terra-cotta

These two doorways in Queen's Gate, London, were designed by Norman Shaw,
and show the progress of his style
from the free use of varied materials (*above*)
to a later and more formal handling of the Renaissance vernacular (*opposite*)

91

The Red House, Bayswater (the one with the shutters)
designed in 1874 by J. J. Stevenson,
was one of the landmarks in the development of domestic architecture.
As usual in such cases, the architect was his own client

Another celebrated house of this period was No. 9 Melbury Road,
a medieval villa designed for his own occupation
by William Burges, the restorer of Cardiff Castle

92

No middle-class Victorian home was complete
without its Minton-tiled conservatory.
This one abuts upon a house in Combwich, Glos

This modish interior, stuffed with the costly caprices
of a fashionable decorator of the period,
is the boudoir of Lily Langtry

The Victorian speculative builder sold his standard residences,
even before they were finished

Our photographic survey began with a building by Charles Barry
and ends with one by his son.
Tower Bridge, designed by Sir John Barry and Sir Horace Jones
and opened in 1894, is an architectural epitome of the period,
expressing in every detail of its picturesque outline
the tremendous self-confidence, romantic yearnings
and technical ability of the Victorian architect